A 3-minute forever book

EAT YOUR PEAS®

for my Daughter-in-law

By Cheryl Karpen
Gently Spoken

A
special gift for you

_____

with love from

_____

At the heart of this little book
is a **promise**.

It's a promise from
me to you
and it goes like this:

If you ever forget what a
wonderful daughter-in-law
you are
or doubt for a single moment
how grateful I am
you are part of my life...

I promise
to stop what I am
doing and remind you
how much you mean
to me.

Meanwhile,
may this little book
help me say
what's on my mind
and
in my heart...

There was
a time when I
couldn't imagine my son
all grown up with
a love of his own.

Now I can't imagine him
any other way!

If it were up to me, I would have chosen you too!

You are special..

And I'm not the only one who thinks so!

Whenever you come to mind, I see an extraordinary, remarkable woman.

Memories
of your
wedding day
will always make me
smile.

Anytime you
want to know
what your man
was really like
growing up,
you have my number.

Want to swap cute stories?

I have a few that might come in handy sometime.

Whatever you dream for those around you, be sure to keep *dreaming* for yourself.

If you ever
need someone to
remind that man
of yours
how very lucky
he is,
just say the word.

I admire you.

Savor each day.
(They pass so very quickly!)

Embrace your gifts.
(You have so very many!)

Be good to yourself.
(Because this mom says so!)

Most of all, stay healthy...

Remember to always
eat your peas...

with the ones you love.

Why Peas?

She was a vibrant, dazzling young woman with a promising future.
Yet, at sixteen, her world felt sad and hopeless.

I was living over 1800 miles away and wanted to let this very special young person in my life know I would be there for her across the miles and through the darkness. I wanted her to know she could call me any time, at any hour, and I would be there for her. And I wanted to give her a piece of my heart she could take with her anywhere—a reminder she was loved.

Really loved.

Her name is Maddy and she was the inspiration for my first PEAS book, **Eat Your Peas for Young Adults**. At the very beginning of her book I made a place to write in my phone number so she knew I was serious about being available. And right beside the phone number I put my promise to listen—really listen—whenever that call came.

Soon after the book was published, people began to ask me if I had the same promise and affirmation for adults. I realized it isn't just young people who need to be reminded how truly special they are. **We all do.**

Today Maddy is thriving and giving hope to others in her life.
If someone has given you this book, it means **you are pretty special** to them and they wanted to let you know. Take it to heart.

Believe it, and remind yourself often.

Wishing you peas and plenty of joy,

Cheryl Karpen

P.S. My mama always said, "Eat your peas! They're good for you."
The tender and spirited words in this book are meant to be nutrition for your heart and soul. Enjoy daily.

A portion of the profits from the
Eat Your Peas Collection
will benefit empowerment programs
for youth and adults.

Genuine Gratitude

I am grateful to
editor, Suzanne Foust
whose passion for words make
every PEAS book unique and special

and to

illustrator, Sandy Fougner
who creatively and lovingly
hand illustrates each page.

A special thank you to my daughter-in-law, Haley Dougall,
for breathing so much life and love into our family.
We love you.

~Cheryl

If this book has touched your life,
we'd love to hear your story.
Please send it to:

mystory@eatyourpeas.com

or mail it to:
Gently Spoken
PO Box 365
St. Francis, MN 55070

About the author

"Eat Your Peas"

A self-proclaimed dreamer, Cheryl
spends her time imagining and creating
between the historic river town of Anoka, Minnesota
and the seaside village of Islamorada, Florida.

An effervescent speaker, Cheryl brings inspiration,
insight, and humor to corporations,
professional organizations and churches.
Learn more about her at: www.cherylkarpen.com

About the illustrator

Sandy Fougner artfully weaves
a love for design, illustration and
interiors with being a wife
and mother of three sons.

Other books by Cheryl Karpen

The Eat Your Peas Collection™

is now available in the following titles:

Daughters	Someone Special
Sons	Faithfully
Mother	Birthdays
Father	Tough Times
Sisters	For the Cure
Grandkids	Extraordinary
Girlfriends	Young Person
New Moms	

Heart and Soul Collection

Hope for a Hurting Heart
Can We Try Again? Finding a way back to love

For more inspiration, Like us on Facebook at the **Eat Your Peas Collection**.
For quotes and pages to post, follow us on Pinterest at
www.pinterest.com/eatyourpeasbook/

To view a complete collection of our products, visit us online at www.eatyourpeas.com

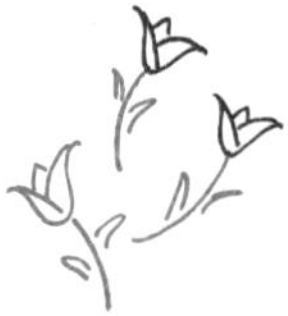

Eat Your Peas® for My Daughter-in-Law

©2007, Cheryl Karpen
New Edition November 2016

Printed in the USA

For more information or to locate a store near you, contact:
Gently Spoken
PO Box 365
St. Francis, MN 55070
info@gentlyspoken.com

Toll-free 1-877-224-7886